**NATIONAL
GEOGRAPHIC**

Turn on a Faucet

Brian Birchall

When you turn on a faucet, water comes out.

How does the water get to your faucet?

The water comes through pipes
in the walls of your house.

How does the water
get into the pipes in your house?

The water flows through big underground pipes that connect to the pipes in your house.
These pipes run under all the streets in your town.

How does the water
get into the pipes under your town?

The water comes from a water treatment plant.
This is a place where water is cleaned.
Clean water is pumped into the pipes
that run under your town.

How does water
get to the water treatment plant?

The water is pumped from a reservoir.
This is a place where water is stored.

How does water get into the reservoir?

The water flows into a reservoir
when a dam is built on a river.
The dam stops the water
from flowing down the river.

How does the water get into the river?

Rain falls from the sky.
The rainwater runs into streams and rivers.

When you turn on a faucet, the water that comes out has flowed a long way!

This is how the water gets to your faucet.

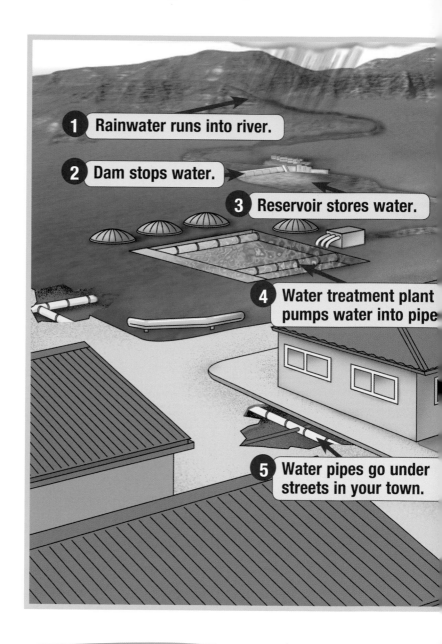

1 Rainwater runs into river.

2 Dam stops water.

3 Reservoir stores water.

4 Water treatment plant pumps water into pipe

5 Water pipes go under streets in your town.

6 Water comes through pipes in the walls of your house.

Glossary

dam   a big wall built across a river to stop water flowing down

faucet   something that controls the flow of water from a pipe

pipe   a tube that water can flow through from one place to another

reservoir   a place where water is stored

river   a large stream of flowing water

water   a clear liquid with no taste or smell

water treatment plant   a place where water is cleaned